SEAMLESS

Publication of this book is supported by a grant from
The Greenwall Fund of The Academy of American Poets.

Linda

Tomol

Pennisi

For Tanya —
with gratitude —
October 28, 06

Linda

SEAMLESS

PERUGIA PRESS
FLORENCE, MASSACHUSETTS
2003

Perugia Press extends deeply felt thanks to the many individuals whose generosity made the publication of *Seamless* possible. We recognize in particular The Fund for Women Artists, our fiscal sponsor, for their fundraising service and expertise. For more information about Perugia Press and to make a tax-deductible donation, please contact us directly or visit our Web site.

Book design by Jeff Potter/Potter Publishing Studio and Susan Kan
Cover image, "Ballerina," a bistre wash and
charcoal drawing on Rives BFK paper, by Suzanne Proulx
Author photo by Mary Stebbins

Library of Congress Cataloging-in-Publication Data
Pennisi, Linda Tomol, 1952–
    Seamless / [Linda Tomol Pennisi].
        p. cm.
    ISBN 0-9660459-6-3 (alk. paper)
    I. Title.
    PS3616.E56 S43 2003
    811' .6--dc21
                                    2003006110

Perugia Press
P.O. Box 60364
Florence, MA 01062
info@perugiapress.com
http://www.perugiapress.com

Acknowledgments

Grateful acknowledgment is made to the following journals in which some of these poems first appeared, sometimes in different versions or under different titles: "Any Weather," "Reddening the Moon," *Bellingham Review;* "Slipping," *Cimarron Review;* "Calling Me," "Wild Field," *Faultline;* "In My Thirteenth June," formerly titled "Wor(l)d," *Indiana Review;* "Poem to My Son," *lyric poetry review;* "Interior with a Girl at the Clavier," *Poet Lore;* "Wor(l)d," "Permanently Settled on Its Rim," formerly titled "Wor(l)d," *Prairie Schooner;* "As We Speak," *Red Rock Review.*

For their advice, friendship, and support, my heartfelt thanks to Robin Behn, Michael Burkard, Cathy Gibbons, Patrick Lawler, David Dodd Lee, David Lloyd, Annie Lugthart, Phil Novack, Julie Olin-Ammentorp, Warren Olin-Ammentorp, Suzanne Proulx, Betsy Sholl, Janet St. John, Mary Stebbins, Leslie Ullman, and David Wojahn.

Special thanks to my family—John, Annie, John, Kathy, and my mother—for their love and encouragement, and also to my father, who died two weeks before news of the book's publication.

Deep appreciation to Susan Kan for her guidance and vision.

FOR MY GRANDMOTHERS

In memory

Annie Rickard Rubright

Mary Herrold Tomol

Contents

1. Wild Field

2. Reddening the Moon

1. Wild Field

What to Do about the Box of Bird Wings
Wrapped in Newsprint from the Twenties

I tape them on, but the still-attached fascia is stiff and brittle and it scratches whatever part of me it touches. Still, sometimes I want my hand to fly. In the worst possible way, I want it to rise up past the O of my mouth and interrupt the slow slippage of air in and out of an ordinary day. Or the part I want to fly is my foot or the extra flesh around my belly. Today, I'm going for the tongue. I select two delicate wings, not quite a pair, but similar in blue-greenness, in size, in curve, in definition. Something zooms from my periphery and smacks against the glass. Just when I've been thinking, *Yes. Perhaps.* Stunned dark wings plummet through the spruce. Who am I to think such things?

Any Weather

Always, a woman in a ditch.
At the age of ten or so a girl
starts to know this. The word
nude gets tied up in it, and sometimes
stabbed or *strangled*. The ditch
could be shallow or deep, filled
with water or trash, sucked into
the woods or curved on the lip
of the thruway. The moment of entry
might be light or dark —
any season, any weather.
And after it snaps, the vegetation
adapts. The girl begins
to understand. Seasons sprout
around her body. The woman
could be a child. Her name
could be Sara or Carol or Jane.
The brush growing up to contain her
might be tender and fresh,
thorny and wild. When her body
is found, it will leave a deep
impression for a while.

Somewhere in a Dark Auditorium

A ballerina will not stop
inserting her small foot
into a slim pink shoe,
crisscrossing silk ribbons
over the bone of ankle.
Sometimes I slip into the inside
of her body, where the soul
wells into the walls that cup
the music, quivering there
like a diver in a swarm
of tropical fishes, her shape brushed
with undulations of hunger
and wonder, a hundred bodies
of tremulous light. The dancer's shoes
fill with flesh; her flesh
brims with music. What can she do
with such hunger, such sadness?
What can her body do
but tremble and spill
into dance?

The Well

She was saying, *In the anterior wall of the well, a blossom
is breaking through.* And he was wondering aloud
how she knew which wall was the anterior. Didn't it depend on
where one was standing in relation to the cement slab, the lid
square but the space beneath it round — they had seen it
once — so that any point at all could be
the anterior? And *wall* to him suggested a flat
space. She might have said *drum,* or *cylinder* or *ring*
and then she could describe the place she was referring to
in relation to clock numbers, and if she were really
exact she could say, *In relation to where I'm standing,
I being 12 o'clock, the blossom is located at approximately 6:33.*
But when he told her this, she began turning into 12 o'clock,
tipping everything into afternoon or a dark new day or just beyond
a brink she couldn't define. He had a hard time keeping her
focused, and she felt it too, always falling into
the dark lens, when what he needed
was for her to coalesce. But for her there was this sweeping
motion where everything kept becoming
everything else. She had thought *anterior* such a lovely word,
and precise. She had struggled for it — the way a painter might
dabble among reds and whites and blues to find just the right
pink, the way a blossom might unfold
incrementally until it might reveal itself
unashamedly in the dark.

Wor(l)ds

Enter the context of fruit
and decision,

the space where the girl,
when asked to play

Mary, replies
in a small

yet ripening
voice, "I want

to play
Eve."

A Question for Narcissus

A pair of cedar waxwings
on the birch's low branch.
With a flair for ceremony
this morning, they keep
passing the same red
berry from mouth
to mouth, female to male,
male to female,
the berry altering,
growing a little redder,
a little sweeter.

I have been told opposites
attract and complement,
yet see how alike
these elegant birds.
Rhythm twins, their sleek
bodies could perch here
all day, caught in kiss

or conversation,
some deep homage
to the mouth.

Muse

I said, I never knew coal black hills
were not a part of every landscape,
at least one mountain of slag rising steeply
at the edge of every town.
The muse laughed.

I was a girl, I carried on,
I did not know I was growing
accustomed to darkness piled
high and immovable,
or spread along the banks
of a creek running through —

a stripe so wide and black
the low fields were lost
to wheat and corn.
The muse fanned herself.

She knew of the gaping holes,
the trash inside them, the cave-ins,
raped girls, lost men.
And the rats — we'd been through
all that — shadowy bodies

emerging in broad daylight,
fighting for scraps in the yard.
More fanning. One long
audible sigh.

And the ditch where our neighbors' sewage
pooled, and the darkness inside the church
where each Sunday my voice soloed into the ear

of the stained-glass shepherd,
where I waited fervently for three hours
once each year for Him to die.
A full-fledged belly laugh.

She knew of the lilacs'
trembling hands. She'd heard the whimpering
roses at the greenhouse dump; she was sick
of the whimpering roses. And the well's

dark mouth, Hades' wet, incessant caresses.
I tried the gold cape
and my years as a nurse. It was all
the same. We both knew it.
The draping. The exposure.
A little death, a little sex. Bodies
in all that darkness
withering. Bodies blooming.

Slipping

I.

He was telling a story of a woman
firmly planted at her front window,
of leopards and tigers
filing by. She'd sharply tap the pane
whenever they appeared.
An act of kindness.
What would wild animals do
on a quiet street if she didn't make them
disappear? All that morning I'd been teetering

on a strand of conversation
about breath, a friend's inability to get
enough of it. Lunching at the white
plastic table, sun heaving
through the glass,

I began slipping into a world
of breathlessness and imagined
animals, and I used the fine lines
around his eyes to pull me back.

II.

Once on the verge of sleep I was a goat
among a herd of goats, sure-footed,
rushing down the rocky hillside
toward some essential gap,
some deep gorge where a warm wind
stirred the poppies and the willows
nodded their heads in an elaborate
gesture of belief.

III.

I am stepping back across two weeks'
worth of words to the round white
table. I am returning to the moment
I asked him to change the subject,
then to the moment I re-introduced
the subject, which for me seemed to be
the fragility of saneness,
the seam between control and its loss.
I am returning to the moment the slipping
began, the moment it subsided,
when I felt steadied not by logic
but by acceptance, by an eye
the color blue the goats
were moving through.

IV.

Standing on the porch
in deep summer, have you ever watched
a train edge across the upper field?
Maybe it was dark, maybe you needed
the piercing sweetness of its headlight,
its slow rumble, the slight tingle
on your soles as you stood barefoot
in your nightclothes, how it tugged
almost invisible cars across the field
like a slow string of words, a sentence
you didn't know would be spoken.
Maybe you relished the slow chug,
the delicious pulse shadowing through
long after the headlight

had passed, while a few feet away,
the Peruvian daffodil trumpeted
its sure white silence into the small
dense garden at the foot of the stairs.

V.

Listen, I'm ashamed to say this,
but once I was approaching a revolving door
and lost my sense of direction. I didn't know
which way to enter the moving glass,
how to slip my body between the panels
so I'd emerge on the other side.
And sometimes driving, if an incline is long
and not very steep, I can't tell
if I'm going uphill or down.
I could tell you other things,
things I wanted to place
in the sunlight before him
on the white plastic table, so we
might shape them into something
that feels a little less like death,
but that would have taken time
and there wasn't enough of it.

VI.

When I entered the farmhouse
and turned on the light, shards of glass
on the blue rug tried to look beautiful,
but the hole in the picture window
resembled a tracheotomy, the shade
sucking against it like torn tissue,

the chandelier dangling like a uvula above.
The house was stirring; a fat wasp
buzzed in its lungs. I didn't know
what to make of the sharp metal object
at my feet, how it had thrust
into the electric room.
Groping with tape and newspaper,
I tried to obliterate mosquitoes and moon,
block out breath and breeze, deny
the full dark space the train
keeps pulsing through.

Rose

I need to understand how flowers
and darkness intersect. I sense
it has something to do

with God. The Tea Rose
for nineteen seasons
has ruffled at my window.

The Grandiflora shows me
each year how to deepen
then bloom. I kneel down before

my Floribunda. Sometimes I call my flower
Angel Face, sometimes Pink Peace
or Fairy. When it displays small,

ornamental hips, I call my flower
Ballerina. When I find it
high-centered, bushy, or cupped,

I say, *Hey, Empress; Hey, Lady;*
Hey, Queen. When it blooms
wildly two-toned and showy,

I call my flower Double Delight.
Each day my landscape aches
with fragrance and death.

This soft-lipped, heavenly secret keeps
spreading petals wide, showcasing
the drop of ambrosia inside.

Suckle

The first syllable
forms the cup

the second's fluid
is meant to fill.

And at the juncture
this bit of sweet, quick work,

like the rake's final pull
of last year's leaves

from the hill
where the spring

prepares to fill the dark,
expectant gully.

In My Thirteenth June

She entered the page where I kept the word *tit*
and the word *boy*. She tore into the deep
pocket of woods, and traveled
the length of my voice
and came to the cavernous place.
At the base of my tongue, in pinkness
and filtered light, she saw the beautiful,
swimming things. My mother trampled
among blood blossoms and blushes;
she found, shaped like her tongue,
the cliffs I'd plummet from, and vines
of sweet fruit, and she peered
into the dark pouch beneath
the cascading forsythia.
My mother lowered herself
into a warm body
of water not meant for her.
That day, she returned a little wild
and shaken. You might think
she'd been searching for her lost girl.
I tell you — I did not know how
or where to place myself
after that. I turned toward
darker pockets, more shadow.
Half the year, I'd vanish
entirely. Half I'd pretend
I was still there.

Sleep

I want to see this
change as other than
drying. I want to see it as new
life and windows thrown
wide and books tossed aside
if they're boring.
I want to keep on living
as if nothing much
is altering. *How ya doin'?*
What's goin' on?

I want to move along
as if absence were acceptable,
unnoticeable, as if till now
my soul has not emerged
from its own cave each month,
has not tongued its red
parables over three decades

of my life, more real to me
than Christ. Then I would not need
to grieve like this. I would not
need to sleep with death's
taste in my mouth, would not wake
steeped in darkness, spreading out.

A Parched Sun Brims the Final Third of Her Life

When (s)he

(with)holds

the scar(r)ed

place, mo(u)rning

(n)ever breaks

Edible Flowers

Sometimes our separate
hungers overtake us.

It was a few weeks after her birthday
and her father's death.

I pulled petals
from the nasturtium, passed some

across the table. We shared
that flower the chef had placed

among the tenderloin and beets
on my plate, wiped up drippings

as if we were used to lingering
in a restaurant with petals

between our fingers, our hungers
wild and delicate that night.

Soon I learned my father too
was dying. Aren't all flowers

edible? They should be. I
would take the whole peony

between my teeth, tear its meat
and its pinkness, pismires and all.

Lovers

after the painting by Kitagawa Utamaro

He places

(at least)   one

of his tongues

inside

(at least)   one

of her mouths.

Syllables

spool,

sounds   flower

like silk.

Transubstantiation

At this junction of sweet
red mother milk cloud
salt father milk she ponders
Jesus and food and
wonders about travel
of the body or spirit
she can't tell which
but would like to ask
him really tell him
a thing or two about
crossings and intersections
arrivals departures
but would he think
her too self-assured
too confused too much
a bother questioning him
from the end or beginning
of a string of blood
her spirit already bitten
and her flesh on its way
now like the inside
color of apple?

Poem to My Son

Fall, 2001

Last night I dreamt you in a dirt cellar.
I dreamt a vein of space inside
the wall and inside that vein I dreamt
your body, not as the small boy
who entered other holes
and came home sweat-soaked
and dirty, but as the body that keeps
you now, almost twenty-two-year-old
body that always and never changes,
and when I woke you and pulled you out
your friend's body emerged behind you,
and behind him another friend,
and then another. In these days
packed with unrecoverable bodies
I call you up from every vein inside
that has been brushed with you,
and every vein has, and then I need
to do what I have always done,
to find the cracked blue bowl
among the others on the shelf
and ladle into it what I have cooked
or peeled or shredded, or whatever
story has sprouted in sleep's
dark root cellar, and then watch
your mouth unhinge to take it in.

Wild Field

I don't know what to say about the field.
I can't seem to make sense of it.
Once, rows of potatoes. And corn.
And yes, the coal-laced border
at the lower end, then,
and still, now. If someone says, *Imagine
a field*, it's this one. And if he says,
*Imagine the neurons in your brain
as a field of grain*, I bring that smothering
overgrowth inside me, the one
slim way out, here. *Create new
pathways, wear down or break
the stalks, part them with anything
but drugs.* I love the vowelly
mourning doves in the fruit trees
at the weeds' periphery, the cicadas
rattling till the jar of evening
empties of silence. In a boat
the same shape as my body, I drift
into the wind's swift whispers,
sink beneath the gods' overlapping
conversations about a small girl
caught in Teall Creek, rushing downstream,
her long panic before she was wrapped
in a series of warm, black coats.
For a long while, she'd shouted, *Help me.*
For a long while, from the petrified banks,
the villagers tried.

2. Reddening the Moon

A Week Away, at Home

The tiles in the shower are coming apart, and the ceiling
beneath keeps blossoming mysterious stains

I try to interpret, waiting for the repairman I still
haven't called. It's spring again: the sky's a full,

ruminative gray, so much joy
just inside the magnolia it's ready to split.

For days now, walking, or cooking an egg,
the yolk gummy and gold at its center, I've been thinking:

This is what it means to be myself. And Easter morning
early, driving toward Skaneateles Lake, the setting

moon on the country road a wide silver mouth
that drew me forward, and for an instant in my rear view

mirror the sun's rising perfectly aligned, myself
part of the bridge between them. *This is what I mean.*

The way my body shapes the space between my mouths
some days, the fullness within like that quiet road —

mist still settled on a small pond, not ready to give up
what happens at night. The cardinal in the cluster of hawthorns

not quite showy, but wearing a color laced with shadow
and brimming light. And this morning, my week's

almost gone. Soon our three TVs will be on,
the phone incessantly ringing, and I will slip

myself inside again like a lover might
tuck one's body back inside each piece of fabric,

his expression painfully loving, as if he might not see
what was breathing inside those dark garments any time again.

Interior with a Girl at the Clavier

after the painting by Wilhelm Hammershoi

To make the day percussive.
To finger the keys, to finger the clear light

flooding the keys, and with that fingering
fill two white bowls with music.

We feast upon whatever song
she has been playing —

whole notes clinging to the bowls'
wide rims, diminuendos

melting over the dish of butter.
Her chair-back fans into harp strings.

Half washed with light,
half soaked in shadow,

she folds the pale blue room
into arpeggios,

holds black and white
together. There is a girl

inside a room.
There is a room

inside a girl.
The interior of music

swells
with music.

In Her Reversible Cape

The girl
picks her way

toward the hospital
on an April morning.

When she spreads
gold wings,

you'll see a shock,
dark there.

Red Running through It

I deposited my first
decade of blood
into small coal towns
in the heart
of Pennsylvania,

and once in Boston
I twirled my majorette skirt,
pleated with white and blood,

and a couple of times
at the Jersey shore
I bled into the rhythm
of hair dye and palm readers
and The Supremes
and the ocean.

Later in a stone residence
among fifty student nurses,
and also in the Ashland State General Hospital
as I bathed and catheterized,
shaved and injected,
I bled.

At twenty, I prayed
for blood in London.
In Cardiff and in Paris
I prayed and prayed
for blood,

and for the next few years
I bled in indiscriminate

places, mostly snowy,
though after a hard loss
once into the striped blue heat
of the Caribbean,

and I may have bled
on an army base
in Champaign, Illinois,
at the home of a high school friend
and her babies
that year in summer.

In my late twenties,
I bled almost exclusively
in Upstate New York,

and I was thrilled not
to bleed in New Orleans,
though the food
was jazzy and the music
rich as blood,

and when I resumed
I kept my blood away
from Pennsylvania for a while
due to Three Mile Island.

Then for two decades
I bled in unnoteworthy places,
though last year in Chicago
I threaded the white space

between the Monets and O'Keeffes,
to the African exhibit
where I bled into masks
and deep drumming.

And just this spring
I bled all the way
from Syracuse to Albany
and back, and in that capital city

I bled underground
in a building shaped
like an egg, and I bled
in a hotel room

and through readings of poems
by men who had never bled
and women who were bleeding too,
and some who had stopped,

and some who had not stopped
but who during those April
days were quiet.

I was succulent
as a pomegranate, warm
as a scarlet coat in a cold window.
Those days, I cupped flame.
I flew. I bled.
I was a rich geranium then.

The Strippings

We called it *the bush*.
Woods, forest came later.
We called the mudholes *ponds*.
The soil, sprinkled with slag,
tried to look glittery.
We called the soil *dirt;* the slag,
we called *coal dirt*.
The boys swam in *The Lily,*
a mile away, and too deep.
We could not swim;
we could float. We'd float
into the bush, around the edges
of holes. The sun flung
a sadness there. We laughed
and played in it. At the Big Pond
we'd float into our muddy faces.
We called the stripping Judy fell into
a *coal hole*. The town took days
to find her, far from her boyfriend's
parked car. *Coal holes* were deep
and lined with trash. She
was an older girl. We
knew not to go anywhere
near them at night.

Field

It's hard to see. This evening I'm walking
Tielman Road. In this part of Pennsylvania
coal fields border corn fields. Black and green
touch and quiver. It is summer.
A train shimmies from the tangle
of trees, pulses across the upper field
like a sentence that has been stuck
in the throat for a long time,
part of the narrative, slow
in its coming. Will it take days
for these reverberations to fade?
A boy in a red pickup
clatters by, and beyond
the kicked-up dust another boy
takes shape, working in the lower field,
growing or harvesting as if his life
depends upon it.

*

From the porch I watch night's dark pieces
slide together, the apple tree in the yard's
deep center urging the woman beneath it
to roam the fields, the woods, undetected.
In the dusky margins of sleep,
Thomas Edison would hold a steely
in his hanging hand. He wanted the dropped
marble to startle him when he drifted
too far, so he might retrieve the dreams
and images there. The porch grows
dark now. A boy is climbing
the stairs. I make room

on the wide seat beside me.
The dark has swallowed;
the boy and I are swinging inside her
full and open throat.

*

Anything could happen. I could die
first. Or I might live my whole life
avoiding darkness, or too much light,
as if the in-between is the right place —
the road distinguishing the upper from lower fields —
a place to walk the dog, jog a little, free of burdocks
and snakes, the mess of abundance:
the tasseled stalks' incessant whispering,
a panic of flashing gold, a rush of disheveled blue.
The pig sty in the patch of woods
at the field's far end, empty now,
requires me to fill its dark
eyes and mouth with memory
or myth, as if the day requires
more than washing clothes, weeding
the garden, burning the trash.

*

There is a boy in a cellar. I know this
because I see his irises from the corner
of my eye. Tomorrow he will emerge
and cross the road, slip into the field,
swallowed by tall stalks there.
He will pick the corn, peddle it
door to door, to the nice
houses. My father peddled coal

he bootlegged with his brothers
after losing their farm. They'd shimmy
thin bodies into deep, tight pockets,
light sticks of dynamite to dislodge the vein.
I imagine my father's mouth and ears,
his blue eyes brimmed with darkness
inside the earth's tight sleeve.
Now eighty, my father's heart
is failing, his vessels so clogged
doctors can do nothing but offer nitroglycerin —
Slip one under your tongue for pain.
And my father begins to shuffle
toward the burial plot he's chosen
overlooking green hills and coal holes.
Along the way he cries,
then smiles. He buys
bushels of peaches, and eats corn
twelve ears at a time.

*

Once a cat lived its whole life
in my grandmother's deserted cellar,
never succumbing to curiosity,
if she had any, about the field just beyond
the high window. The door to the kitchen,
always ajar, never drew her through. My father
drove to Florida one year and returned
with a truckload of fruit.
The trip up the coast was long,
his truck packed with perishable globes
of light. From then on, he didn't travel
far from home. In the webbed

darkness of my cellar, dusty jars — trapped fruit
nudging wide-eyed inside them,
fraying sacks of grain, decaying bodies
of rats. In the bin coal shifts,
clinks with its own glittery weight.
Always, a blue-eyed boy deep
in one corner, figures a way to keep food
in the mouths of his sisters. Steps away,
a field rises goldly along the road;
an underworld tugs just beyond it.

Eve

The birds' voices pitch high,
a little wild, forecast
the snake. Far away
from my body, a naked woman
wrapped with serpent, mouths
deliciously attached to the small,
imperfect apple.

Some days I want to study
the angle of the mouth when it's hungry,
I want its darkness, the sad way it tries
to eat the light.

Some days I want to see
inside, understand the chewed fruit's
path as it slips downward. Essence. Oblivion.
The rub of flesh on flesh, the color
of hunger, the color of fullness,
the color of the semi-permeable
membrane between.

Once there was a woman.
Then there was a man. Once a woman
bought a skirt of snakeskin print,
but did not know it. She had seen
it as cracked eggshells. Delicate.
Neutral. When her husband said,
Snakeskin? she removed it.
She did not know she had slipped
into the fabric of change.

At the Heart of the Garden

World of mouth: f(e)ast

world of palm: s(k)in

world of fragrance: (b)rain

world of iris: (c)leaves

world of ear: gull(y)

Permanently Settled on Its Rim

It was like a burning bush; I needed
to keep going there to listen
for the red voice.

It was like gold; the poor boys
followed me around all day.

It was the whole note, middle C;
all my songs were played around it.

It was an empty pop bottle, green
and dirty, beneath the forsythia.

It was a new mouth
required to contain
a meaty hunger.

It was the nub of the tulip.

It was like a billboard the high school
boys were suddenly obsessed with
signing.

It was the deep
hole near the clothesline
where the rat slept.

It was a buzz, a shimmer, a hum.

It was my first tranquilizer,
my slow pink pill.

It was the tender spots inside
being chewed monthly.

It was all words containing m's
and vowels and n's.

It was the strip-mined hole; the nude
girl dead inside it.

It was a drawer —
my first black bra
wickedly balled
beneath pink panties.

It was the miniature orchid
I secretly salvaged
from the greenhouse dump.

It was the pocket of woods
I'd enter when I was afraid.

It was afternoon. It was May.
It was afternoon.

It was the boy next door
home from seminary,
entering his sister's
sleepy room to leave something
wet on her stomach.

It was the loss of Sunday swims
with my father.

It was the word *lick* or the word *lip*
or the word *linger*.

It was a church organ
playing Amazing Grace
at the touch of a button.

It was my mother
pulling on her raincoat
of silence.

It was every object in my sad
and cluttered room
briefly bursting
into something golden.

It was a nest with a bee
permanently settled on its rim.

Recital

Imagine them dancing,   or pretending to

dance.   The cool darkness backstage,   in the wings of the stage,

in the laps of mothers who fill wooden chairs — it covers their hands

like winter gloves.   Imagine two golden-

sequined girls moving in a ring

of light.   Darkness so thick

they cannot hear   the music, if there is

music.   Imagine them turning   together

as if they are still friends.   They pliée.   One shadows

the other's arabesque.   As if nothing happened

in the small girl's kitchen when she and her mother

were away,   as if her father

never called the tall girl

inside.   See their eyes   lidded with blue,

and how their backs   press together,

their   outstretched   arms

joined at the hands.　Even now one is bending

forward,　holding the other on her back.

They are like one stalk covered with too much rain, a stargazer lily

heavy with half-bloom,　facing down.

The Morning after the Dance

In the kitchen, the boys are taking down
my daughter's hair. They look sleepy
and slow, fingers fumbling

among bobby pins and blood
red rosebuds, her gold-
brown curls unraveling like a story

rooted just beneath
her flesh, face framed with the mess
of disheveled detail. So much happens

in a kitchen — summer rain
taps the glass, a girl grows,
cries or laughs, depending on whose

clumsy chariot idles in the driveway.
Filmy goddesses slip in
and out of the fluorescence,

check pears for ripeness, the freshness
of eggs. Today they huddle around
the mound of purse-shaped buds

on creamy Formica as I scrub
the vegetables and husk the corn.
I'm weary of pomegranates

and narcissi. Wanting new stories
to mingle with the old, I invite
the goddesses to help me write one

over tea. We agree: we'll use this
girl, these two tall boys,
the laughter they bring back

and back, the small mountain
of kiss-shaped buds, this
simmering water, the deep,

fruited cups we sip from, this...

Communion

Because she trembled. Because her fingers
could barely slip the small glass cup
from its silver hole in its silver tray.
Because of the way she'd make
those shamed seconds audible —
the clinkclinkclink as she returned
the cup — she turned away
from the altar's sporadic, purple
offerings, which is why she is always
hungry, see, her mouth
open as the altar's cut lily
in its golden vase, the lily cupping
each sacramental minute. Who said
those who kneel at the curved
rail for this brief moment, swallowing
small cups of deep fruit
are more blessed than she in the field
who cannot ever stop
studying the mouths
of flowers?

Morning Prose

Burgundy your fingers. Point your toes. Enter the grief inside three inch heels. Wobble a little. Be wordy or throaty. Be story, be memoir, be speechless if you want. Arrange the light around the flute into an opus or an art piece. The indigo bunting will pick seed at the base of the feeder. Tie her in later, or invite her in now. Dress in a painting. Cross your legs over the day. Summon a butterfly to hatch in your hair; she will hear herself singing. Go on and on and on. Babble. Ramble. Unravel. Reveal. Lose your mind on the stucco ceiling; find your heart in a box on the floor.

Wednesday Afternoon

Today all the men
who have touched her breasts
have come for tea.

One is talking with his mouth full.
One gets up to play
Hey Jude on the piano.

One, still pretty much a boy,
sits wide-eyed and sullen. One sets up
his drums on the deck.

One kicks a football in the yard;
for a moment all their eyes
look skyward. One of the men is talking

of the deep, secret places framed by stars.
As if moved, another strokes her leg and asks:
Do you want me to say I love you?

The blonde is playful; he likes the slow
peeling of bras the color of fruit.
Opening all the doors of her cupboards,

one searches for extract of almond
or vanilla; tea is bland, he says,
without it. Curled at her feet, the girlish

man wants her hands in his hair.
One pulls a prescription pad
from his white breast pocket.

Don't worry about me, she says, I have a full
day ahead. The tea is brewing. The house
is stocked with food, with music.

Forgive Me for Not Loving the Lei Enough

The tuberoses'
petaled connections
do resemble birth,
and lip my breasts
with the moon's
fairest yellow.
Yet this sharp
sweetness
slips too deep
beneath
my breathing
to mean anything
beautiful.

As We Speak

for Mary

In a downtown café
we read poems of pomegranates
and desire. Around us
men in business suits strike deals,
toss scores of ballgames,
stock market quotes. What is it about

words on the page that makes us
lean together like this?
What turns the buildings
rising solidly outside
into tall women in gray
slender gowns?
They are taking the sky in their mouths
as we speak; their ancient shoes
form underworld pockets of ashes
and flame. Listen.

Sometimes I can't tell if I'm living
or dying. Sometimes my voice
rises out of me like a fountain;
sometimes it cowers in my throat
like a sick angel. Or like Eurydice,
it succumbs to a glance, then retreats
into shade. When I was a girl

peaches clung to the tongue-tied tree
in the backyard, small-cheeked blushes
welling up from somewhere deep.
Yesterday in a half-empty auditorium
a violin sprouted from the curve

between a young woman's shoulder
and tipped chin. The bow

in her hand, held steeply, pierced
the half-dark with quick,
violet screams. When oblique,
that bow tongued the strings
mournfully, emitting the song
it was all along meant for,
a low moan of love,
shame or bliss.

Night Shift, the First Time

Hanging her cape on a hook,
the girl goes humming
room to room. In the far lab,

the cat in its blue plastic bag
does without her fingers
this week. Down the cool

corridor, a urine-soaked man
cries out; a death
rattles and moans. O the boy

right now crossing Ashland Mountain,
the boy in his Chevy Impala,
driving home. He must be entering the weak

stretch of road where the mine fires
slip their long, smoky exhalations.
She imagines him blasting

Satisfaction into the full summer night;
she can almost hear him
singing. And he is drumming

hard on the wheel, the girl
knows it: all his windows down,
and the taste of her still

lining his mouth, and his voice
projecting out, and sulfury
moonlight silvering in.

Lost Shoes

Leaving the hospital, it was I
who could not find my way.
I was steadying her
down the long, stark corridor,
aware of nothing but her
pale bare feet, her toenails
midnight blue and iridescent,
as if torn bits
of what had been
the sky were blowing
in slow gusts across
the dirty tiles.

When in that deep, bewildered world
the black E-X-I-T painted tall
on the white swinging door
lost its meaning,
it was my daughter,
head somewhat cleared
of vodka, who pointed me
toward it. I remembered then

that it was night
and it was snowing —
my car two far
lots away. I wanted
to be large enough
to carry her across.

Closing the Door at Night

I sometimes listen one last
moment to the yard.
The dark is such that I lose
all that's behind me — piano

and tables and bowls, the television's
thick blue drone, the leather chair
cradling my husband's awake body.
Sometimes he calls me away

from the open screen, as if among
the rotting apples a reclining angel
pulses gusty wings, waiting.
How to say what night means —

my soles' need for the threshold's
ridged impression; my face and breasts
inching into all that surrenders
hard edges. To be swallowed by wingbeat

in wet grass, where caving fruit releases
its no longer bearable sweetness.

Reddening the Moon

For Effie

On the balcony, with the moon
stuck to her shoulder. No.
On the balcony, with the moon
blooming from her mouth.
And her red shoes doing what —
dancing? And her red shoes
reddening the moon's blueness,
like her red shawl whitens her breasts
as they gleam there in Chicago,
October, early '70s, and almost thirty
years later when asked, *What*
does the moon remind you of?
my friend remembers this: her friend's
flesh, the photographer's flash,
and the moon low and sultry,
rounding its way to a glossy page
in Spain, the shoes high-heeled
and highlighted, her friend's
body a river shimmering
from shoes to moon, moon to shoes,
the dark that night vivid
and lipstick lush. And though tonight
as we walk this wide circle
atop this wide hill, the moon
so full we feel it pulls us
to the world's rim, we know the dark
may never be that lush again,
but our faces glow a little
and our pace slows as if our feet
have stepped into the color
most worth remembering.

Echo

This is another story: she lived
near the fields, communing
with the sheep, the dark shepherds.
At one time she had a body,

but you know how it is when the gods
get involved — nothing remains the same.
Trees change shape and the entire
field rises up but in the end, it cannot stay.

He pitched a longing too haunted
for soft sheep and mild shepherds.
He pierced all things
of the field with his song:

tall grasses collapsed, the wildflowers
thrashed their tongues brightly,
indecently, and the sheep
ran rings around desperate shepherds

who could not contain them.
The god pressing, pawing the air
just short of her, while the shepherds,
too, turned part animal,

and the sheep spun dizzily,
and the throats and hearts
of all involved tightened
with the heat of mid-September,

with everything crying.
Anything might happen: panic
could turn into madness,
a warm body could tear apart,

could end up merely a memory,
an image of a few bright flowers,
a mouth repeating something
deeply familiar from afar.

Things I Want to Say before I Stop Blooming

Rose me.
Tulip me.
Peony me.
Poppy me.
Daisy me.
Orchid me.
Dahlia me.
Azalea me.
Hyacinth me.
Lupine me.
Rhododendron me.
Sweetpea me.
Portulaca me.
Magnolia me.
Snapdragon me.
Trumpet me.
Rose me.
Rose me.
Rose me.
Rose me.

Ballerina

after the drawing by Suzanne Proulx

The costume dangling
in the afterdance coolness
looks infused with her. The tights
a remnant — *pas-de-chat?* — on the verge
of collapse, the entire figure
delicate, skeletal, as if the dance
has coaxed out the dancer's
inner skin, as if the pose
closest to her bones pulses here
in the halfdark, centripetal flesh
capable of miracle, or of retaining a lover's
exact shape for that first instant
after love. Now the costume's pelvic chamber
glows as if the dancer has left
a lamp on, and she has,
the skirt a curtain sheer enough
to sift the dance out, to let
the emptiness shadow through.

About the Author

Originally from Pennsylvania, Linda Tomol Pennisi lives in Syracuse, New York, where she teaches in the Creative Writing Program at Le Moyne College. Her poems have appeared in journals like *The Evansville Review, Prairie Schooner, Bellingham Review,* and many others. A former nurse, she earned her MFA in Writing from Vermont College.